Mingling in the CIA:

Observations of an Underdog

Shelly Mateer

Characters in this book are fictionalized and loosely based on a compilation of characteristics that the author has observed.

All statements of fact, opinion, or analysis expressed are those of the author and do not reflect the official positions or views of the CIA or any other U.S. Government agency. Nothing in the contents should be construed as asserting or implying U.S. Government authentication of information or Agency endorsement of the author's views. This material has been reviewed by the CIA to prevent the disclosure of classified information.

Preface

My life has changed dramatically for the better after leaving the Central Intelligence Agency. I can now look back on the sometimes torturous period I spent working there and laugh more than I cringe. Most of all, I feel a huge sense of relief at having escaped that world. In publishing my observations, I aim to shed some light on a career that few know much about, while also hopefully entertaining some people and possibly even offering hope.

I will always remember the words of my first supervisor upon being granted my very first Top Secret clearance. He said that having a Top Secret clearance was like "having an albatross around your neck". While I believe he was using the expression incorrectly, he meant that with holding a Top Secret clearance comes certain responsibilities and expectations. The people of the CIA are entrusted with our national security, and are supposed to be held to a higher standard than the average citizen. They are the "cream of the crop", paid with taxpayer money. In reality, many of them typically act no more mature than pre-teen children at their worst.

Starting out as a new employee of the CIA, entering the strange bubble in which I would spend the next eight years of my life, it did not take me long to identify some very distinct personality traits characteristic of the people working for the Agency. While I acknowledge that these personalities can likely be found in *any* workplace, in the CIA these characters make up the vast majority of one's colleagues. The Agency seems to draw them like a magnet. In some cases, perhaps the CIA environment creates or highlights the negative traits of these people.

Names and certain identifying characteristics have been changed.

The Five Most Common Personalities

1) The Frazzled Woman

2) The James Bond Wannabe

3) The Shapeshifter

4) The Prisoner

5) The Blacklisted

1) The Frazzled Woman

Ms. Frazzled is a woman I was to become very familiar with during my time in the CIA. She is typically unmarried, perhaps divorced or on the road to a divorce, usually in her forties or fifties. This woman can be observed most naturally in her cubicle habitat frantically scurrying about, talking in fast, tight-lipped sentences that usually revolve around how busy she is. An expert at playing the martyr, this woman is a master at creating chaos and instilling a sense of urgency in all office matters, no matter how trifling they really are. She can talk your ear off and leave you wondering why you didn't turn and run when you had the chance. She is prone to office meltdowns, occasional sobbing spells, and is an overall mess. She is also strangely obsessed with what she eats. She can spend hours discussing every bite of food she has consumed in recent weeks, days or hours (conveniently omitting the copious amounts of anti-depressants she inhales). Always receiving exuberant accolades and abundant monetary awards she is quite skilled at fooling upper management into believing her skills are no less than phenomenal. These women are usually, if not always, placed in management positions where they can torment the lower-level officers into hating their jobs. Characterized by a penetrating scowl, blotchy skin, and a huffing and puffing as she rushes everywhere filled with blustery self-importance.

Karen

Karen was my first manager in the Directorate of Operations (DO). I was introduced to Karen after she blew off our required lunch meeting during CIA 101, the orientation class for all new hires. The idea was that someone from your new office would meet you one day during the class, to help introduce you to your new job. Sadly, I don't think Karen ever even realized that she had missed this appointment, as I'm sure she was much too involved in telling people how busy she was to meet with a new employee. Karen was likely hired because her husband was a bigwig in another directorate, and she spoke many languages. Her husband would often call her at her desk and bark out orders and insults, only then to end the call by hanging up angrily on her. These phone interactions always left her looking demoralized, and I felt sorry for her. One day I had the misfortune of answering one of his calls when she was not at her desk, and his anger issues were apparent even in that brief phone exchange. While I pitied her for being married to such an arrogant ass, Karen was so overwhelmed by her own importance that she failed to train me on any skill that was required of a Staff Operations Officer, and I spent much of my first assignment doing endless name traces, and corresponding via email with any kook who decided to contact the CIA through their public website. She certainly did not want to do these tasks herself. When our famously temperamental Chief of Station (COS) retired, Karen wanted nothing but to position herself to go on a trip to our much sought-after European Station. She spoke of all the shopping she could accomplish. Our new COS was a very well-groomed, easy-going guy who would visit our little cubicle corner every once in a while before heading out on his posting. Each time he dropped by Karen nearly had a stroke from nervousness while trying desperately to impress this man. At the time, I had no interest in going on a trip to this country. You can imagine how Karen's jaw dropped when one day he nonchalantly turned to me and asked when I would be visiting his Station. I passed on the opportunity, mostly because I was on my way out of that position, but also to give my younger co-worker a chance to go.

Denise

Just a few seats away loomed Denise. Denise had a permanent scowl on her face. She was a super skinny Frazzled Woman who was completely obsessed with telling everyone about whatever she had eaten that day between critical outbursts about anyone and everyone. She also loved to gossip. Denise had ears like satellite dishes, so she was able to pick up practically any conversation in the office and then repeat it to you word-for-word. This skill could come in very handy in the intelligence community, but was sadly misplaced and unnecessary in the cubicle world that we lived in. Denise was an expert at giving unsolicited advice and she never forgot a perceived slight. I am forever haunted by her tales of a love affair she had with a married Agency man who loved to suck on her toes. Denise was nearly impossible to end a conversation with. I spent many a morning prisoner to her never-ending questioning and frequent rambling about the above-mentioned toe-sucker before I learned to avoid walking by her cubicle all together. Denise was particularly interested in any man who showed even a hint of interest in me. Male visitors to my cubicle were a source of intense scrutiny from Denise, and upon their exit I was promptly interrogated about my relationship with these supposed gentlemen callers. She was convinced that any man within a mile radius of my presence had amorous intentions, despite my many objections.

2) The James Bond Wannabe

I had the misfortune of meeting many of this type while at the CIA. A James Bond Wannabe is usually a twenty-something-year-old with visions of James Bond dancing in her head. These young women (I had more exposure to the female version) would saddle up to you upon first meeting, appearing to pursue a friendship. They could sometimes even appear helpless, and one might be tempted to take them under one's wing. But beware, Ms. Wannabe is on a mission to fast track through the Farm and feels she needs to prove what a great intelligence collector she can be. Mentally never having left high school, she will attempt to learn any personal information, perceived weaknesses, and secrets you may have so she can report them back to anyone who will listen. She is a formidable gossip at her finest and a professional backstabber. Characterized by wide eyes, a friendly smile, and an inappropriately timed wink.

Natalie

Natalie was a tall platinum blonde who wore her hair in an interesting beehive hairdo and tragically applied eyeliner on each upper lid that looked as though someone with a shaky hand had taken a sharpie to her face. Natalie was hired during the big push to increase the number of officers under a different type of cover. Attempting to change the Cold War method of intelligence collection, the CIA sought to increase the number of officers under non-official cover, but it didn't seem to matter if the recruits had any relevant experience or if they could manage to get them placed overseas effectively. Natalie was one of many hired just out of college, with absolutely no work experience. She was a Midwestern girl who had not seen much of the world. While her wide eyes and friendly grin made her look open and innocent, her six inch spiked heels hinted of something else. She was a mean spirit underneath. She rarely had anything nice to say about anyone, although she was always sugary sweet to everyone's face and had a hard time saying "no" to anyone. One of Natalie's favorite hobbies was office gossip. She would spend her entire day chatting on the chat messenger we used in the office, gathering what I'm sure she thought was "intelligence" on her co-workers. Natalie was on the fast track to get to the Farm and complete her operational training, all sponsored by our Group Chief who was completely enamored with her. Power hungry, Natalie strove to position herself near any man she perceived as powerful in the Agency hierarchy. When a single COS took a liking to her, Natalie jumped on the opportunity to further her career by whatever means necessary. It mattered little that his appearance revolted her.

A ruthless backstabber, she was the true "tip of the spear".

Annie

Annie was not as attractive as Natalie, so she did not have as much access to the powerful men of the Agency. She concerned herself mostly with co-workers. Annie was someone who made you constantly question the hiring process at the CIA. She had absolutely no knowledge of world events and no sense of reality. She would frequently come to work after a night out on the town in DC, with tales of being followed by foreign intelligence services. All it took was one conversation at a bar with a visiting Frenchman to convince Annie that her every step was being monitored by the DGSE

(France's external intelligence agency). She used the computers in the office to participate in online dating, never questioning her decision to use government computers to arrange her latest hand job. She had never matured past high school (I've actually met eight-year-olds more mature than her). She was a failure at her job and tried to redeem herself by digging up information on her co-workers and "friends" and perhaps even reporting them to the Office of Security. (I was once lucky and careless enough to fall victim to this!) I am convinced she did this in order to persuade management that she would be a good case officer. Her light, cooing manner of speech was only slightly less annoying than her propensity to read between the lines of anything anyone ever said to her, twisting each conversation she had into something completely inappropriate and somehow sexual. Annie considered herself a very bright girl, and she was on an endless quest to prove it. The scariest part about Annie was that the Agency knew she had psychological issues and should not be there, but they preferred to "pass the trash" and shuffled her from meaningless job to meaningless job as a way to *not* deal with her. Until enough time had passed that short memories would prevail and she would be placed in an overseas station where she could do the most harm to national security.

3) The Shapeshifter

The Shapeshifter can be found working at either Headquarters or in the field, and when he goes on TDY travel, he becomes a different person. His motto is "what happens on TDY, stays on TDY". Frequently married with children, Mr. Shapeshifter promptly forgets about his family life upon boarding the plane for his Agency-sponsored travel. Once freed from his domestic constraints, he can be found in the nearest seedy bar or chic nightclub chain smoking (a habit that he reserves solely for his travels) and drinking to complete inebriation. Then it is off to pick up a prostitute or stripper for the night. Anyone who knew him at home would not imagine that he smoked and drank as much as he actually did, much less guess that he frequented hookers. Likely bored with the mundane aspects of his job (this boredom is heightened when Mr. Shapeshifter is based out of Headquarters); he seeks to create the excitement that the daily tasks of his job lack. Typically Mr. Shapeshifter is involved in operations, and sometimes even works as a case officer, which contributes to his confusion and double life. A person who lies for a living can have difficulty separating reality from fantasy, although he is usually not self-aware enough to recognize this. Characterized by average looks and a slight, almost imperceptible glint in his eye.

Kevin

Kevin was a case officer who would TDY frequently to the beach area where I lived for a case that we worked on together. Kevin and I became friends after I thwarted his numerous attempts to sleep with me by convincing him I was a lesbian. I had become particularly adept at this little trick over the years of dodging perverts inside and outside of the Agency. I suppose my little charade was the reason he felt comfortable enough to share his atrocious behavior with me. Through many nights drinking heavily at various bars he would entertain me with his tales of debauchery until the wee hours of the morning, at which time he would slink off with the woman he had picked up earlier that afternoon. This guy was quite the multi-tasker. I could never figure out how he found the time between our afternoon operational meetings and our nighttime bar visits to find these women, but he never failed to deliver. Kevin spoke very little of his home life, and I quickly learned not to ask. I knew he had a wife, a small child, and another one on the way. That didn't stop Kevin from having a woman in every port. He would smoke like a chimney, drink like a fish, and then slither off to his latest mistress. I'm not sure if Kevin had been exposed to that lifestyle in the foreign country he was posted in, and had adopted it for himself, or if he had always been this way. He did not smoke when he was at home playing the perfect family man, but as soon as he stepped off the plane in the States, his first task was to buy cigarettes and a lighter. Grabbing some condoms (these were strictly for appearance, he did not often use them), off to the bar he went! His foreign trips went much the same way, with the only difference being that he strictly preferred the local hookers in those countries.

4) The Prisoner

This poor soul began working for the CIA just out of college, and has never had any other employment. With hopes of an exciting overseas career that were dashed after some years of Agency service, The Prisoner's only remaining wish is to make it to retirement and get out of the Agency. However, this type usually never manages to escape from the Agency's clutches, and after he retires he will end up returning to work as a contractor, to spend his days hunched over a computer in a cubicle at Headquarters. The Prisoner dreams of having a hobby or a second career to turn to in retirement. He secretly admires those around him who participate in outside activities that are not Agency-related, but he himself does not have the courage, creativity, or energy to come up with his own ideas of activities he would be interested in. He frequently has an exact countdown of how many years, months, days and minutes he has left until his retirement, and when asked how he is doing by well-meaning friends, he will happily recite this information. The Prisoner is

trapped in a cage of his own creation. Characterized by a dull, hopeless look in the eyes and a
bitter smirk.

Chester

Chester was a soft-spoken type who was at a point
in his Agency career where he did not enjoy any of
his recent positions but did not have any hope of
getting posted overseas before he retired. His
retirement was not too many years away, but not
close enough. Chester openly admitted that he did
not know what he would do with his time once he
retired. He had no hobbies or outside interests. He
knew that the lure of money would likely draw
him back into the Agency as a contractor for
another disappointing, soul-sucking job upon
retirement. Having spent all of his working life in
the CIA, he really had no other options - he had no
job skills relevant to working outside of the Agency. Chester was prone to developing crushes on
women he worked with, typically women who
were completely out of his reach and league. He
would spend his office days attending an endless
procession of meetings and chatting on the messenger system with his latest crush, a woman who
likely had no clue of his feelings for her. Chester

would escape, but only for a brief second. He would retire and relish his moment of freedom, only to realize that he *needed* the cage of the CIA cubicle. With the help of a hungry government contractor, he would be placed right back in his cage within weeks of retirement.

5) The Blacklisted

This CIA character could be anyone at the Agency. One could start out at the top of the Agency world, a so-called golden boy, and suddenly become an outcast. This unfortunate person has been black-listed for some reason by someone who decided to make it their mission in life to discredit them and make it nearly impossible for him/her to get promoted or, more often, to get any position they have applied for. I met and befriended many of The Blacklisted during my time in the CIA. Prior to meeting each one, I would hear stories about what many of these people had supposedly done wrong in the past (the deed that their career would never recover from). While there was always a shadow of mystery surrounding what created their tar-nished status, some of the worst offenses one could be brought down for were either involving finances or sex. True or not, it did not matter, once the charge was levied, it was permanent. It was called a "hall file" - a mysterious record of the bad behavior that even The Blacklisted himself had no idea about. Anyone who was less inclined to think for themselves would believe the rumors, but I have always had a soft spot for underdogs.

After all, I was one.

There are some good people at the CIA, but they typically get beaten down early on and then proceed to be chewed up by the system. More commonly you will find people who have either become warped by the strange world that they have grown accustomed to, or perhaps they entered on duty as an already soulless human being.

The CIA culture is a unique one. I have held many jobs in my life, but I have never seen such a concentration of negativity, maliciousness, and paranoia confined to one place of employment. We were always being told how workplace satisfaction ranked extremely high at the CIA, based on the surveys we would occasionally find in our inbox. I'm not sure where these happy employees were, but this was not the same CIA that I knew. I was surprised to find that the CIA, which prides itself on hiring and attracting "the best of the best", could, in reality, be so dysfunctional.

I learned to recognize these personality types and did my best to steer clear of the soul-sucking ones, not always successfully. If you find yourself in a poisonous situation, surrounded by these characters, whether a relationship or work environment, take comfort in the knowledge that you *can* get out! You will need a thick skin and a strong sense of self, but you can do it. It will take time, but with patience and vision you will escape. Plan ahead, develop some outside interests, keep your wits about you, and remember, always *be nice*. Be human. Even when surrounded by unpleasantness, never give in to becoming one of the callous.

About the Author

Shelly Mateer is a former CIA officer. She studied International Relations at the University of California, Davis. Shelly grew up in various U.S. locations and overseas. Her first book, *Single in the CIA*, is a memoir about her experience working in the National Clandestine Service (aka Directorate of Operations) of the Central Intelligence Agency. She currently resides in Southern California with her husband and son.

More information is available at
www.shellymateer.com.

Want to see Annie in action? Turn the page for a sample of the next book in the *Mingling in the CIA* series.

An excerpt from *Mingling in the CIA: Annie.*

What was the big deal?

She had only missed two intelligence reports that were supposed to have been relayed to Station. Annie looked across the table at her scowling supervisor, Marisa. Seated beside Marisa was Sean - maybe he would have some sympathy. Annie pursed out her lips to a pout and widened her eyes, giving Sean a coy smile from across the table. Sean caught her eye and looked away, embarrassed.

Okay, so maybe my feminine charms won't work on Sean. He must not like girls.

"Annie, this is not the first time you have let us down. Station is relying on us to get these intels to them in a timely manner. This is *wartime intelligence*. There are no more crucial intels than these," Marisa shook her head disapprovingly. Gathering her papers, she knew there was nothing she could do to get through to Annie. Annie was just another person hired out of desperation and placed in a position she had no qualifications or aptitude for. This was happening more and more these days.

"Just be aware that a note will be placed in your file regarding this incident." Marisa knew as well as anyone there was no "file" besides a hall file.

Annie already had an atrocious hall file. Marisa walked briskly out of the room, Sean following behind her like an obedient dog.

Annie grabbed her latte, swung her beaded wrap around her shoulders indignantly and trudged back to her cubicle. *I need to find a new job*, she thought. Flashing on her computer screen was a chat message from Carina. She wanted to meet in the cafeteria. Annie had already bought her over-priced coffee, but she didn't have anything better to do.

This war can wait! I need my biscotti.